The Freshman "Secrets" Handbook

A Secret Survival Guide to the First Year of College

A "Gift Card" Handbook

By
Tammy
and
Scott Vineyard

Copyright © 2013 Tammy And Scott Vineyard

All rights reserved.

ISBN-10: 0615758274

EAN 13: 9780615758275

May you experience all the joys
that life has to offer

To:

From:

"Going" Forward

This is not some high psychological profiled rendition of years of studying "Freshman."

This is also not a step by step "Follow these rules or fail" guide to freshman year.

We have seen these books and they are too complicated for our purpose.

This book is for the friend or relative that wants their Freshman to have all the tid bits they need to be successful that first year.

This book is for Freshman, written by two authors who not only "Survived" but…

Got the T-shirt, put it on backwards, took it off and tried to put it on again inside out!!!

Basically, we wanted your freshman year to not reflect the "OOPS, I should have done this" or "OOPS, I should have done that" game we played.

I wish someone would have told me this stuff!!!

Enjoy

Tammy and Scott

The Secrets to Getting Started

Stay in a dorm room the first semester to meet new friends and beat the commute.

Do not go home every weekend, stay on campus and find things to do.

Do not take a maximum course load during your first semester… Enjoy Life

Do not take an 8am class everyday. Sleep in some days

The Secrets to Getting Started

Signing up for a credit card to receive a free gift is NOT recommended.

Bring some things that remind you of home but don't be afraid to express yourself when decorating your room.

Look online about teachers and classes prior to registration.

Make sure you sign up for a recreational class that interests you… volleyball, tennis, bowling, etc.

Find a place on campus you can call your own… under a tree or beneath a statue… and Relax.

Freshman Secrets

Go to all freshman orientations

Go to all free food functions. You'll meet new people, maybe learn something and get a belly full

Check out the fitness center and join/participate. Avoid the dreaded "Freshman 15"

The Secrets to Getting Started

Call your parents, grandparents or family once a day… They are terrified!

Ask Questions!!!

The Secrets to Getting Started

Get on a meal plan

Don't play your music too loud… Negative attention will get you nowhere.

The Secrets to Getting Started

Be <u>Nice</u> to everyone you meet.

Map out your classes before the first day. Know where you're going.

The Secrets to Getting Started

Flip-flops are a must, everyone needs a pair.

Freshman Secrets

Buy, read and re-read "Financial Peace" by Dave Ramsey. It's a must.

Secrets to Social Life and Meeting People

Meet your neighbors and befriend them.

Go to a sorority or fraternity rush.

Secrets to Social Life and Meeting People

Be willing to let go. Find everyone interesting.

Find a church, Synagogue or other place that shares your spiritual beliefs.

Secrets to Social Life and Meeting People

Smile and be polite.

Be respectful to others. Yes... Be respectful to others.

Secrets to Social Life and Meeting People

Don't be judgmental. Not everyone dresses the same, listens to the same music, or has the same interests.

Be the person who always gets the door for others.

Secrets to Social Life and Meeting People

Keep your opinions grounded. You don't know everything… Listen

Always use good manners, the ones that would make your Grandmother proud.

Go to parties but be responsible. Make wise decisions.

A taxi is always more desirable than a jail cell. "<u>Never</u> drink and drive."

Secrets to Social Life and Meeting People

There is always something to do… make time for studying and "you time."

Your best satisfaction will come from being a good friend. Let your heart be open and always giving.

Make close friends and treat them special.

Freshman Secrets

Have a movie night with friends. Don't forget the popcorn!

Secrets to Social Life and Meeting People

Start now. Keep a calendar and address book of friends and family. Never forget a birthday! It means so much!

Not everyone will like you. That's okay. Be nice.

Secrets to Social Life and Meeting People

You won't like everyone. That's okay. Be nice.

Freshman Secrets

Give to others. Giving is the essence of life.

Secrets to Social Life and Meeting People

Secrets to Fun

The best fun is giving. Find a charity and volunteer yourself and your friends' time. You'll be amazed at how much fun this is and how close it will make your friendships.

Go to a water park with friends.

Secrets to Fun

Smile… and be polite.

Freshman Secrets

Learn a joke and tell it. But never let someone you know be the butt of a joke.

Laugh and laugh a bunch.

Freshman Secrets

Go to your school's sporting events. Paint your face and yell for your team. Even if they stink.

Parties are great but be wise. It's your choice but make good decisions. Take a moment before deciding and follow your heart.

Music puts the mind at ease. Find some time to relax and enjoy your favorite tunes.

Secrets to Fun

Because of its importance, it's worth repeating… Give some of your time to a charity.

Go hiking! You + Nature = FUN!

Secrets to Fun

Spend time with your Grandparents and/or your Parents. You'll soon learn the importance of family.

Play cards.

Secrets to Fun

Have your friends over, make popcorn and watch scary movies. Don't worry about the furniture. They came to spend time with you not your possessions.

Get friends together and play volleyball, kickball, etc…

Secrets to Fun

Buy a bike and ride around campus. Feel the wind in your hair. You don't need people around you all the time to have fun.

Go on a date with someone you enjoy talking with. Who knows where it might lead?

Go to a tailgate party and cheer for your team.

Have a cookout. Grill something!

Secrets to Fun

Go to a dance. And Dance!

Before going on break for the holidays, have your friends over and have your own Thanksgiving and Christmas.

The Secrets to Studying

Ask questions in class. You won't understand everything, guaranteed.

Freshman Secrets

Don't monopolize the classroom. Your teacher has office times for a reason.

The Secrets to Studying

Sit in the front of the class. Don't feel like a loser, you'll be the winner when you learn more.

Don't be afraid to audit a class. Some subjects require a second look.

The Secrets to Studying

Visit the library and absorb the knowledge.

Don't be afraid to read ahead if the subject interests you. Your teachers will hate it but it will keep you involved.

The Secrets to Studying

Don't procrastinate; all projects have timelines. Think how relieved you'll feel when you don't have to rush to get things done at the last minute.

Record your teacher's lessons. Replay them before you fall asleep, you'll be amazed at how much is retained.

The Secrets to Studying

Study groups are an important part of being successful. If you feel you don't contribute, bring coffee or baked goods. There's a place for everyone in college.

Memorize, memorize, memorize. Some things are worth retaining forever. (Please Excuse My Dear Aunt Sally)

The Secrets to Studying

Don't just take classes in your major. Take courses that interest you.

Even if the subject doesn't interest you, take a teacher that does.

The Secrets to Studying

Exchange notes with other classmates. People really do hear differently.

Don't study all the time. Balance is important.

Find a restaurant like Denny's or Waffle House, or a coffee shop like Starbucks where you can study late. Coffee is your new best friend.

Classes are only as good as the effort you put into them. The more effort = the more you learn. (P.S. You are there to learn.)

Studying sometimes stinks but great grades and knowledge rule. So do it already.

Sleep with your books/notes under your bed. Osmosis works for plants, it just might work for you.

The Secrets to Studying

Cramming works but studying a little bit each day will allow for more retention of information.

Go to your local planetarium, museum, and/or zoo. Be in awe of the world.

The Secrets to Studying

The Secrets of the Simple Nature

Buy, read, and re-read "Everything I Need to Know I Learned in Kindergarten" by Robert Fulghum.

Be open-minded. You are about to be introduced to different people and cultures. In life, there is no room for bigotry.

Be spiritual. Your choice… just be.

Freshman Secrets

B reakfast is the most important meal of the day… so says everybody.

The Secrets of the Simple Nature

Embrace positive role models like Oprah or Bill Gates. Read a non-fiction book each month.

Your friends are not your measure for success. You should determine your own worth.

The Secrets of the Simple Nature

Try to walk or bike ride as much as you can around campus. It may be easy to bum a ride but your body will thank you for the extra exercise.

Spend time outdoors. Sitting in your dorm room watching TV and eating junk will not benefit your overall growth. Go outside… remember sunscreen.

Your advisor should be a friend interested in your goals and aspirations. If not, find another advisor.

Learn to cook a few of your favorite dishes. You will want a home-cooked meal every now and then.

The Secrets of the Simple Nature

Donate to charity or volunteer for community service. Yes, it's that important.

Spend time with family whether it's going home to see parents/grandparents or hanging with siblings. Family really is important.

Working while in school builds characters but remember to balance school, work, and play.

Take up a hobby that will help you grow as a person.

The Secrets of the Simple Nature

Remember, you're an adult now. Adults think before they act… at least, the ones that make good decisions and stay out of trouble.

Dream, Imagine, Create.

The Secrets of the Simple Nature

Anger is a necessary emotion at times but it's also needless most of the time. Get past it quickly and try to move onto a more rational emotion that will help solve your problem.

Teach. You may not work in a school or run a corporation but always find ways to help others learn.

Hope, Dream, Love, Faith, Integrity, Caring, Character, Giving, Trust, Honesty… Should all be words you try to live by in your life.

You are about to inherit the world. Learn from its accomplishments and mistakes. Always stay true to yourself.

www.ingramcontent.com/pod-product-compliance
Lightning Source LLC
LaVergne TN
LVHW051845080426
835512LV00018B/3071